CONTENTS

C000274078

Shere and Gomshall lie on the eastern side of

BLACKHEATH HUNDRED*

DOMESDAY BOOK – 1086

This is a translation of the abbreviated Latin in which it is written.

ES-SIRA (SHERE), in lordship. Queen Edith held it.
Then it answered for 9 hides; however, there were then
16 hides* there. Now it does not pay tax.
Land for 14 ploughs. In lordship 2 ploughs; 19 villeins* and
6 bordars* with 12 ploughs. A church; 6 slaves. 2 mills at 10 s;
meadow, 3 acres; woodland (assessed) at 50 pigs.
Value before 1066, later and now £15.
In Wotton Hundred the King has 3 virgates* in lordship which lie in
(the lands of) Shere and are assessed there.

GUMESELLE (GOMSHALL), in lordship,
Earl Harold held it.
Then it answered for 20 hides, now for nothing.
Land for 20 ploughs. In lordship 2; 30 villeins and 8 bordars
with 18 ploughs.
6 slaves. A mill at 40d; meadow, 3 acres; woodland (assessed)
at 30 pigs.
Value before 1066 £15; later £10; now £20; however, it pays £30.

The villeins of this place are exempt from all the Sheriff's concerns.

The Bishop (of Bayeux) wrongfully placed half a hide of the land
of this manor in the manor of Bramley, and holds it; it was in
Gomshall before and also after 1066.

In Wotton Hundred the King has 1 hide in lordship which lies in
(the lands of) Gomshall..

EARLY HISTORY

Es-sira (Shere) and Gumeselle (Gomshall) were two of a series of settlements in the Tillingbourne valley, along the stream that was vital to their existence. Their arable land lay mainly to the south, on the greensand*, while sheep grazed the chalk slopes of the downs to the north and meadowland was in the valley bottom. In the Hurtwood further to the south were woodlands which provided timber as well as food for pigs. South of the greensand ridge were the heavy, but productive, clays of the Weald. East-west tracks ran along the valley and the downs, while many north-south tracks ran across the North Downs and the river and then through the Hurtwood to the Weald.

The Domesday survey of 1086 is concerned with the vill* of Shere, stretching from the top of the North Downs to the present Sussex border and containing some 30 households. The vill of Gomshall, which included Peaslake, covered a similar area with over 40 households. The number of inhabitants quoted for each settlement also encompasses the area now respectively in the parishes of Cranleigh and Ewhurst. Most of the men were villeins, tied to the soil and working on the lands of the Lord of the Manor, but also with plots of land they could work for themselves. The others were bordars doing casual work, and so poorer than the villeins. Slaves, or serfs, were part of the Lord's household.

The meaning of the name 'Shere' has been interpreted in different ways; either indicating 'a part that was cut off from a larger whole' or, more simply, describing the clarity of the stream. Gomshall is more straightforward; it means 'Guma's shelf', or the level piece of land belonging to the Saxon, Guma. Peaslake refers to the stream where the peas grow.

Medieval ploughing

DEVELOPMENT TO 1850

The early settlements of Shere, Gomshall and Peaslake and their scattered farmsteads were based on agriculture and agricultural products. All tenants were subject to manorial customs of dues and inheritance. The 1380 Poll Tax gives evidence of an active community engaged in spinning and weaving the wool of the sheep; fulling* and tailoring the cloth; tanning the skins and making the leather into boots and harness. The vill of Shere was divided into two manors in 1297 and in 1309 the Lord of one of them was granted the right to hold a market and an annual fair. This was a sign of prosperity. The market would have been held in the centre of Shere, now known as The Square. Some family names in the 1380 Poll Tax are familiar as property names today over the whole area of Shere, Gomshall, Peaslake, Ewhurst and Cranleigh. A few houses still standing have traces of construction as early as the 14th century but 1550–1650 was the most active period of building and rebuilding. There were weavers, mercers* and clothiers owning or occupying property in the 17th century, although the

3

cloth industry based in Guildford was in decline from about 1550. Emmanuel Bowen's map of Surrey (1753) shows "Famous for Weaving of Fustian"* over Shere and Gomshall. Seventeenth and 18th century deeds show many men holding an acre of land "in the common [open] field". (See Farmlands page 8) Agricultural trades were the predominant occupation until the coming of the railway in 1849.

THE CHURCHES

The Domesday survey shows that there was a church at Shere in Saxon times, but there are no visible remains of this building. The present church, dedicated to St. James, dates from the 12th century. There are Norman features but it is mainly Transitional* and Early English*. It is near the centre of the village, looking over The Square and is beside the Tillingbourne, with the principal farm house, now High House, behind it. Alterations and restorations have been carried out from the beginning of the 13th century until the present day.

St James' Church by B.W.Leader

St. James' Church nave

The Lych Gate, designed by Edwin Lutyens, was built in 1902, commemorating Mrs Marjorie Warren, née Bray. Notable ancient features are the quatrefoil and squint in the north wall of the Chancel. These were the apertures through which the anchoress* Christine, daughter of William the carpenter, made her contacts with the church. In the 14th century she lived in a cell built against the north wall of the church, enclosed there by her own wish (details in the church pamphlet).

Brass in St. James' Church, Shere. Translation of Latin inscription at base: "Here lies Sir Robert Scarclyf, once Rector of this parish, who died October 25th, 1412. On whose soul may God look with favour. Amen"

Church records go back to about 1500 and include inventories, names and accounts of church wardens and rood* wardens and bequests to church and parish. The names of rectors are known from 1270 and the parish registers start in 1547 (details in the Church booklet).The patron of the living was the Abbot of Netley (Southampton) from 1243, but the patronage was granted to the Brays in the 16th century, after the Dissolution. It has remained with them, except for an interval of some 150 years. After it was sold by the fourth Edward Bray in 1676 to

Thomas Duncomb, five Duncomb rectors followed the first Thomas until the death of the last Thomas in 1843.The first identifiable parsonage for the parish of Shere was situated near the Tillingbourne to the west of the village. John Evelyn of Wotton dined there in 1677; John Aubrey had visited it during his 'Perambulation of the County' four years earlier. He describes it thus:- "Here is an extraordinary good Parsonage House of old Timber building, encompass'd about with a large and deep Mote, which is full of Fish. Without the Mote is a Canal, wherein are the best and biggest Carps that ever I saw; and tho' they be in the Mote, yet (the river running) they are more properly river Carps: It is also famous for good trouts". This house fell into disrepair and was pulled down and replaced by the present 'Old Rectory' which was built further back from the Tillingbourne in 1844 and enlarged in 1859. A new and smaller rectory was provided in the Spinning Walk in 1950.

St. Marks Church, Peaslake

There is a daughter church at **Peaslake**, designed by Ewan Christian. It was consecrated on St Mark's Day, 1889 by the Right Rev. Dr. Harold Browne, Lord Bishop of Winchester. A burial ground for Peaslake on Ridge Hill was given by Reginald M. Bray in 1889 and a year later the Lych Gate designed by Arthur Blomfield was erected.

United Reformed Church, Gomshall

Gomshall has a **chapel,** built in 1821 and enlarged in 1887 for the Congregationalists. It is now part of the United Reformed Church and is linked to URC Dorking. Regular services are held.

The local **Roman Catholic** community met in individual houses for Mass until after the Second World War, when a Nissen hut was donated on a site beside Station Approach, Gomshall. It was known as 'the tin chapel' and dedicated to 'Our Lady of the Angels'.

Our Lady of the Angels, Gomshall

After much hard work raising funds, and many gifts, enough money was raised to build the present church which opened in 1964. It is served by the Franciscan Friary at Chilworth. Some inhabitants of Shere parish were members of the **Irvingite** ('Catholic Apostolic') movement, which built a church in Perpendicular* style in 1840 on the western side of Albury Park.

The house named Quakers Orchard in Peaslake may have included a Meeting House for **Quakers** in the parish. The Seman family, local landowners, are known to have been Quakers.

THE MANORS

The north-south extent of the Domesday vills of Gomshall and Shere has already been described. On the east, Gomshall bordered with Abinger; on the west Shere included part of Weston in Albury. Shere and Gomshall were both royal manors. Prior to the Norman Conquest, the manor of Shere was held by Queen Edith, wife of King Edward the Confessor and the manor of Gomshall by the King. He was succeeded by Earl Harold. After the Conquest, both were held by William I. In 1086 he granted Shere to William de Warrenne, who had married his daughter, and been made Earl of Surrey. Gomshall remained in royal hands until 1154. Under the Plantagenets (1154-1485) both manors were divided.

Shere Vachery

By 1300 the properties in Shere manor had been divided between two of the sisters of Richard Fitzjohn, son of John Fitzgeoffrey, Lord Lieutenant of Ireland (who is thought to have had a 'capital mansion' in The Square in 1258). The larger part became known as 'Shere Vachery et Cranley' from its manor house of Vachery in the southern part of the manor which went to Joan Butler; her descendants became Earls of Ormond. It was held by the Ormonds for some 150 years until the attainder* of the fifth earl in 1461 following the defeat of Henry VI. It was then granted by Edward IV to John Touchet, Lord Audley, to whom there is a memorial brass in Shere church. His son James joined the Cornish rebels protesting against Henry VII's taxes and after their defeat at Blackheath in Kent in 1497, he was beheaded. Henry then granted the manor to his minister, Sir Reginald Bray, in 1498.

Shere Eborum*

The lesser part of the manor went to Richard de Burg, Earl of Ulster, son of Aveline, Richard Fitzjohn's third sister. It descended from the Earls of Ulster to Edmund Mortimer, Earl of March and then to Richard, Duke of York, hence the name Eboracum or Eborum*. It reverted to the crown on the death of York's widow, Cecilie. Henry VIII treated it as part of 'the Queen's Portion' and it was settled on his successive queens, from Catherine of Aragon to his fifth wife, Catherine Howard. Sir Edward Bray, nephew of Sir Reginald and already the owner of Shere Vachery, purchased Shere Eborum in 1547.

Gomshall Netley

The Gomshall manors were granted to Cistercian religious houses. West Gomshall was granted to the Abbey of Netley in Hampshire in 1243, whence it derived its name of Gomshall Netley. On the dissolution of the monasteries, Gomshall Netley was granted to Edward Bray in 1537, subject to an outstanding lease to John and Thomasina Redford (an earlier John Redford of Shere who died in 1516 is commemorated by a brass in Shere church).

Gomshall Towerhill

In 1389, East Gomshall was given to the Abbey and Convent of St. Mary of Graces, near the Tower of London, founded by Edward III in 1351. From this ownership it became known as Gomshall Towerhill. It was granted to the statesman Sir Edmund Walsingham in 1539, and sold by him to Sir Edward Bray in 1549.

Continuity of Bray Ownership

The manors have remained in the Bray family, except that Shere Eborum was sold in 1609 by the third Edward Bray to William Risbridger who already owned its principal house behind the church. The Risbridger family owned it until 1723 when they sold to William Wakeford of Bramley. His son sold to Thomas Page of London in 1760, but in 1771 William Bray bought back both the manor and the demesne lands*.

The Manor Houses

The manor house of **Shere Vachery** was on a site of that name, south of Cranleigh, though nothing remains except traces of the moat. Joan Butler is known to have lived there around 1300. In the 16th century the Brays resided there and also at neighbouring Baynard's, and at Towerhill, Gomshall.

Shere Eborum's principal house was the farmhouse rebuilt about 1630 and later called High House. William Bray (1736–1832), Lord of the Manor from 1772, lived for a time at Hawkins in Upper Street called The Great House on a 1772 estate map and now known as Old Manor Cottages. The Victorian Manor House was built in 1844 by Reginald Bray, a second son of the Lord of the Manor, and was called Firhill until about 1888.The Bray family has since moved to High House.

High House, Shere

The manor house of **Gomshall Towerhill** dates from at least the 16th century. It was owned by Sir Edmund Walsingham followed by the first Sir Edward Bray. It is said to have been lived in by the second Sir Edward in the period 1560–80, when he was not at Vachery or Baynards. His son Reginald, who married Elizabeth Roper, grand-daughter of Sir Thomas More, probably inserted the chimney in the old part and ceiled over the original hall about 1600. The main part of the present house was built as a new wing in1600–1610, probably by the third Edward Bray after his marriage in 1603 to Jane Covert of Twineham, Sussex. The Bray family continued to occupy until the death in 1803 of

Towerhill Manor, Gomshall

William's elder brother, the Rev. George, the then Lord of the Manor.

The original **Netley House** seems to have been a farmhouse on the site of the present Netley Farm. It was also known as King John's Lodge. It may well have started, in the 13th century, as a grange, or farmhouse for the monks of Netley Abbey. The Cistercian order was particularly interested in farming and had a class of lay brothers engaged in farm work. This Netley House and the Netley demesne lands were sold in 1640 by the third Edward Bray to his brother-in-law William Heath of Piddinghoe, Sussex. In 1682 they were bought by Peter Hussey of Sutton Place, Abinger, and the whole estate was acquired by Edmund Shallett in 1751.

Netley House, 1965

The present Netley House was built about 1790 by Edmund Shallett Lomax (grandson of the above) as a replacement for the mansion of Sutton Place which was then demolished. Netley was rebuilt and enlarged about 1860 by his granddaughter, Mrs. John Fraser, after a fire had gutted the interior. It is now owned by the National Trust but is not open to the public.

It is thanks to the continuity in manor ownership that very substantial manor records have been preserved.

The Bray Family Coat of Arms

ESTATES AND FARMLANDS

Estates

In the eastern part of the parish bordering on Abinger, the Sutton Place estate held much of the land. The Husseys, merchants from London, added the Netley (West Gomshall) estate to it in the 17th century. The Towerhill Manor estate (East Gomshall) extended south to Burrows Cross. In Shere the High House estate had its property both north and south of the village.

Further to the south, between Shere and Gomshall and the Hurtwood, lay several important farms, the present Ponds Farm, Cotterells, Hound House, Quakers, Lane End Farm and Hazel Hall. In the 19th century, the greater part of this area became part of the Goldhawks' Hazel Hall estate; some of it derived from their relatives the Woods. This estate was sold to the Cubitt Trustees in the second half of the century. Meanwhile, the Lomax family had extended the Netley estate in the Hoe area of Peaslake. Much of both these estates was broken up and sold or leased for residential development in the first quarter of the 20th century.

Farmlands

The main medieval open fields of Shere and Gomshall, divided into strip plots, lay to the south of the villages. Many of the strips were bought by William Bray at the end of the 18th century. There was another open field to the north of Shere.

Woodland on the downs above Gomshall bears the name 'the Kings Wood', referring to its early association with Edward the Confessor.

There are extensive manorial and common lands, now mostly woodlands, particularly in the Hurtwood, south of Shere and Peaslake. In 1926 Reginald Bray dedicated the Hurtwood manorial and common lands to the public for 'air and exercise'. While the Lords of the Manor retain the rights to the timber and stone, the public has access to some 5,000 acres, belonging mainly to the Bray Estates and the neighbouring Albury Estates. The Hurtwood Control Committee was formed post 1926 to look after the rights of the public and worked informally, financed by local subscriptions, until 1979. It was then organised rather more formally so that financial grants would be easier to obtain.

RURAL TRADES

Agriculture

All skills and trades necessary for rural living were practiced throughout the three villages. There were craftsmen and tradesmen connected with farming and horses; blacksmiths, wheelwrights, collarmakers or saddlers, coopers, millers and maltsters. In Shere, the main smithy was on the south side of The Square at Gallants for at least 200 years run by the families of Nye, Bignold, Longhurst, Jelley and Upfold, from 1668 to 1878, when the

Wheelwrights

building was converted into a grocer's shop. There was another smithy in Upper Street, where Burrowdown is now, belonging in 1766 to Francis Skurray, a Guildford brewer. William Puttock, living at Bodryn in Middle Street, is described in 1855 as a smith, so he may have had a smithy at Forge Cottage alongside, thus accounting for its name. In the 19th century, Hersey's wheelwright business occupied a large part of the property called Stiles in Lower Street, later divided and known as The Old Forge, and Ash and Willow Cottages. The last wheelwrights were the Hookers who were there from the 1880s to the 1930s. The Hunts were wheelwrights and gunsmiths at June Garden in

Upper Street for about 100 years to 1850. The names of several collarmakers or saddlers located in Lower Street are recorded: Frost, Sherman, Morland and Buchanan. In Middle Street Thomas Langrish's saddlery and Charles Baverstock's smithy continued into the 20th century. At Bignold's in Upper Street the Ede, Street, Crouch and Bignold families were coopers from about 1670 to 1820. When the mill at Gomshall closed in 1950 the miller, Maurice Egerton, started a business in Queen Street, making archery targets. This was continued by his son Robin until it closed in Gomshall in 1998. There are now two houses and office accommodation on the site.

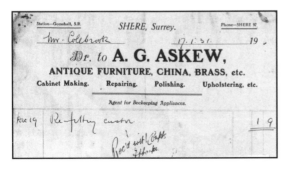

9

Lavender

Lavender and other flowers were grown and distilled for perfume in Shere from the 1920s until the demands for agricultural land in the Second World War took priority. This rural trade was established by the Colebrook family. Lavender House in the Square was run as 'The Lavender Lady' tea shop from the 1930s to the 1950s. Flowers were grown on part of High House farm and the lavender in the fields to the south. There was a still at the farm, and the perfume was marketed under the name 'Essira'.

Fields of lavender

The Cloth Trade

In the Middle Ages, the Guildford area was celebrated for the manufacture of cloth. The Poll Tax of 1380 for the vills of Shere and Gomshall lists 37 spinners, twelve weavers, three fullers and sixteen tailors. Shere and Gomshall were known for the weaving of fustian. This fitted into domestic and small-holding activities with their seasonal demands for labour. The more important men in the trade were the clothiers who organised the supply of raw materials and the marketing of the finished cloth. One such was John Parkhurst of Speers, member of a prominent

Medieval Spinner

local family (also associated with Hound House) and another was John Mabank, clothier and tailor, who owned considerable property in Gomshall and Shere. Mabank and his son combined their trade with sheep farming between 1570 and 1620.

Several families of fustian weavers appear in the 17th and 18th centuries. John Stonell or Stonehill and his son Edward followed the Parkhursts at Speers from 1603 to the middle of the century. John Kelsey and his descendants owned Knaveshurst (Denton) and Gibbles (Elm Cottage), both in Upper Street, for most of the 17th century. Today, Elm Cottage is again the house of a farmer and weaver, Tony Reid, whose family has farmed in Shere and Gomshall for three generations. There were also a number of tailors' premises in Upper Street between 1600 and 1800. Mercers were associated with Shere between 1650 and 1750; John Fawkes, a mercer from Guildford, owned Hawkins (Old Manor Cottages) 1694–1715. John Holland at Speers in the 1740s and 50s was succeeded by his cousin Edward Parkhurst: both were mercers.

Fleece combing

Mills

The Tillingbourne flows from the northern slopes of Leith Hill to the Wey at Shalford, a distance of only eleven miles but its steady flow has powered many mills in the valley (see *The Tillingbourne Story*). **Gomshall Mill** was an important part of the demesne lands of the manor of Gomshall Towerhill in the 16th century. It belonged to the Brays, and may well have been on the site of the mill at Gomshall mentioned in the Domesday survey. The present buildings however are 17th century or slightly earlier.

In 1611 there is a record of a corn mill and malt mill, but by the end of the 17th century the building contained four corn mills. It was sold by the Brays in 1759 to the tenant, David Harris who sold to Thomas Withall of Fetcham in 1786. David Harris must have prospered as a miller; the inventory attached to his will shows that the "chamber over the kitchen" is furnished with a walnut bureau, a mahogany card

Gomshall Mill

table and six ash chairs. In 1839 the undershot water wheel was redesigned as an overshot wheel, using cast iron instead of wood. Nineteenth century owners were William Southon, the Kelseys and from 1897 George Egerton. He sold to Sir Reginald Bray in 1902, a resumption of Bray ownership after 150 years. Mr Egerton and his nephews remained as tenants until 1950. A little later it ceased to be a mill, although the water wheel survives, and after conversion by Mr Wilton of Guildford the building became a popular gift shop and restaurant. It is now a restaurant only.

Several owners of Gomshall Mill lived in Shere. The Harris family lived at Gibbles (Elm Cottage); William Southon, mealman and shopkeeper, lived at Pantry's in The Square about 1830–1850 and also owned a bakery at Vaughans.

At the time of the Domesday survey there were two mills in the vill of Shere. Neither site can be positively identified today. One may have been on the site of the present **Netley Mill** and the other just upstream from High House, or perhaps one was to the west of the village, on the boundary with Albury. The 'Gothick' style of Netley Mill was created by Edmund Shallett Lomax between 1789 and 1793. It continued in operation during the 19th century and the miller, William King, built a house for himself at Gomshall in 1826, now Grovers Cottages.

Netley Mill

The Tanneries

These were important in Gomshall from at least the 16th century. Records show three tanneries in the 18th century. At the Old Tannery House (King John House) there are visible traces of the tanpits in the garden. It was acquired by the Bignold family from Cobham in about 1550. Under their ownership it continued to operate until

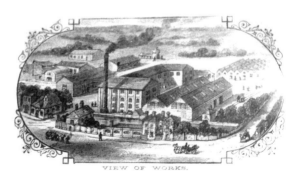

the end of the 18th century. Another tanyard at Loves (9–12 Queen Street) belonged to a 16th century house and also operated until the end of the 18th century.

The third tannery, which survived until the end of the 20th century, was south of the Tillingbourne, with related buildings along the main road. It belonged to the Goddards for most of the 17th century, the Coes for the 18th and William Johnston from 1815 to 1835. Then it was owned by the Eversheds and from 1880–1909 by Gilligan & Son of Reading. Union Cold Storage, later

Cleaning hides

Union International, owned from 1922 when it was still dealing in heavy leathers. As Gomshall and Associated Tanneries from 1948 it became world famous for producing sheepskin garment leathers in a wide range of colours and textures. After sale to Strong and Fisher in 1988, it was closed the following year and the parish lost its major employer. A retail shop was opened in 1973 next to the Tannery to sell goods made from their own leathers; this closed in 1996 and now there is a Veterinary Centre in its place (see *A Tannery in Gomshall*). The tannery site has now been developed for housing.

OLD HOUSES AND FAMILIES

Old Houses (See *Old Houses in the Parish of Shere* for details).
There are several houses in the parish showing traces of 14th century construction but the main period of rebuilding and new building took place in the years of prosperity from 1580 to 1640. Many were timber-framed and most remain today. Several open hall houses dating from 1450-1550 were built with the hall flanked by a two-storey parlour section at one end and a two-storey service section at the other. Chimneys and upper floors in the hall section would have been added around 1600 .
The principal old houses, High House in Shere, Towerhill Manor and King John House in Gomshall are brick-built Jacobean houses, the last two with earlier parts surviving. Those in Peaslake, such as Quakers Orchard and Hazel Hall, were re-fronted in the 18th century.

King John House

The farmlands to the south, extending to what is now the village of Peaslake and including the early hamlet of Hoe, contain a number of old farmhouses dating back to the 1450-1640 period. At the south eastern side of the parish there was a Tudor house standing in the valley leading to Holmbury St Mary. This was Sutton Place (see page 8), a mansion house, with a group of houses built about 1650.
A workhouse was built in Peaslake in the 1720s to accommodate the parish poor until, as a result of government policy, it was sold in 1836 and indigent parishioners had to go to the Union Workhouse in Guildford (later St Luke's Hospital) (see booklet *Shere Poverty).*

Families
Family names can be found in the Surrey Taxation Returns (Fifteenths and Tenths)* of 1332, the Poll Tax of 1380, the records of churchwardens since 1500, the parish registers from 1547 and the Elizabethan muster rolls. There are more names to be found in the manor court rolls, rent rolls, wills, conveyances, leases, accounts and on gravestones.

Prominent families in the parish responsible for building and expansion in the villages include the names Bignold, Bray, Cottell, Francis, Goddard, Hill, Lawrence, Mabank, Parkhurst, Redford, Sands, Sayer, Sherlock or Shurlock, Stonell, Stone or Astone and White in the 16th century. The Amey, Chennell, Gatton, Hussey, Risbridger, Seaman, Slarkes, Snelling and Street families were active in the 17th century.

Population

The population of Shere, Gomshall, Peaslake, Ewhurst and Cranleigh is estimated to have been about 200 at the time of the Domesday survey, and grew only slowly in the following centuries, interrupted by the outbreaks of the Black Death in the 14th century. There were 433 people over the age of fifteen recorded in the 1380 Poll Tax but tax evasion was common. In 1548, for Shere and Gomshall only, there were 260 adult church members indicating a population of perhaps 400 which grew to about 550 by 1724. In the first national census of 1801, the population of the civil parish of Shere is recorded as 871 and the population rose steadily to over 2,000 by 1891. Since then it has grown to some 5,000, reflecting the national trend.

SHOPS

Since at least 1762, Speers, the old property on the north east corner of Middle Street, has accommodated shops and other businesses. The early store keepers were Jesse Attree (1763–89), followed by Coe, Buchanan and Franks (Surrey Trading Company). Early in the 20th century this shop became the headquarters of the Forrest Stores, a pioneering chain of grocers' shops operating throughout southern England. Solomon Sutton (1797–1844) was a grocer who owned several properties in Upper Street. The Smithy in The Square became the Sanders' grocery, in business there for nearly a 100 years from 1878. A shop at Fernside in Upper Street was kept throughout the 19th

century by the Misses Tewsley, James Richbell and Mrs Mary Weaver. It was continued by the Weller family from 1917 to 1973. A small shop was kept by the Batcocks at Manor Cottage in the 19th century and until the 1920s. There was a butcher's shop at Smiths in Lower Street (Old Forge) from before 1758 until 1794. The Bristows were butchers in Middle Street from 1796 to 1853, then moved to the croft of Knaveshurst in Shere Lane where they had a slaughterhouse. They were succeeded there by Edward Farhall in 1874 and by the Dartnells (tenants of High House Farm) in 1890. The Dartnells seem to have moved the shop to the present Lavender House in The Square where it was run by their son-in-law, John Jay. The Read family (originally O'Read) had their shop and slaughterhouse at Hangman's Croft (Seaforth Cottage) in Gomshall Lane for three generations during a large part of the 19th and 20th centuries.

13

The greengrocers (and formerly fishmongers) in The Square was run for many years by the Grover family and since by the Collins.
There was a bakery in part of Stiles in Lower Street belonging to John Sherman in the middle of the 19th century and another in The Square run by the Vaughan family until 1949. Shere's first village Post Office was at Vaughans (see page 19). Gomshall had the Co-operative Stores in what was later the Tannery Shop, also in Bridge House by the railway arch in the early 20th century.

LOCAL SERVICES

Medical Services

Eighteenth century account books of the Overseers of the Poor for the parish of Shere make several references to small money payments for families "in sickness". There are also payments to neighbours who are "tending" them, or providing care. Cases of smallpox and 'traffic accidents' are recorded; there is an instance of a young man "killed by a wagon".

In 1830 there was an agreement with Mr Davey, surgeon, to provide care for poor parishioners "inside and outside the workhouse". For £25 pounds a year, the doctor would attend and supply medicines, including vaccinations, to those residing within five miles of the parish church. There were agreed rates for setting broken bones according to the limb affected and the severity of the break. The top rate was five guineas (£5.25) for a compound fracture of the thigh.

In 1908, a committee was formed under the chairmanship of Dr Cory to set up a local District Nursing Association, affiliated to the Surrey DNA. A District Nurse was appointed and made her visits on foot or by bicycle. Her salary (£90 p.a.) and all expenses were covered by voluntary subscriptions and recourse to local charities. Only subscribers to the Association qualified for treatment on payment of a small means-tested charge. The nurse was found "furnished rooms without attendance" and later, a cottage. The nurses were welcomed and must have worked hard to cover the area. There was sometimes a plea to make "a pony or donkey cart" available for visiting more distant cases. This arrangement continued under a succession of dedicated voluntary officers of the committee until 1951 when administration changed with the establishment of the National Health Service; henceforth the service of the nurses was free of charge.

Until the middle of the 20th century, the majority of General Practitioners worked independently, receiving patients in a dedicated room in practitioners' own homes. In 1960, Dr Stent had a surgery and dispensary built on land adjacent to his house in Spinning Walk, Shere, from where a group of doctors could work as a team, with support from nurses and receptionists. In 1993 this was superseded by a new medical centre and pharmacy in Gomshall Lane.

Dr Isaac Rising Cory (1860–1945)

A history of Shere wouldn't be complete without a comment on a unique man who gave so much to the village. When first qualified he came to Shere in 1886 and continued as medical practitioner (doctor) until 1926. But he was much more than a village doctor. Indeed, he was one of the most vital members of the community, so well loved that the parishioners bought him a car. This was in the late 19th century and a man had to walk in front with a red flag. As a committed Christian he was elected Churchwarden in 1908 and remained so until 1922. He was a most able wood carver and made the reredos for St James' church (since removed). His interest in music ensured he became choir master and in 1905 he helped start the Leith Hill Music Festival. He was also passionate about scouting and, in 1908, formed the Shere troop, the first in Surrey. He also established one of the earliest companies of the Church Lads Brigade. There is a plaque to his memory in the chancel of Shere church.

Fire Service

The Fire Station in Middle Street, Shere was built in 1885 to house the pump, uniforms, brass helmets and other equipment of the Shere and Albury Voluntary Fire Brigade.

The brigade was manned by local tradesmen, alerted by the bell in the turret of the building. The men used their own horses or those from Mr Weller's stable opposite. The brigade disbanded in 1921. The old Fire Station was made into public toilets in 1977.

The Fire Station in Gomshall was built behind the Tannery in 1971 and staffed mainly by the employees. It still provides a service to the community as a Retained Fire Station.

Shere & Albury Voluntary Fire Brigade 1909

Water

The water in Shere village came from shallow wells and was of poor quality (in contrast to Peaslake, where the water was very good). From 1894 some houses in Shere were supplied with water by the Shere Manor Water Co., pumped from the Tillingbourne in Lower Street and near High House. From 1903 the Hurtwood Water Co. took over Netley Mill, using it to drive the pumps and by 1931 the Company supplied water over a larger area than the Shere Manor Water Company. An office and house made of stone quarried in the Hurtwood was built beside Netley Mill. In 1952 the Guildford and Godalming Water Company took over both local companies, built a new pumping station and sold Netley Mill. To encourage water-bird life in this area, the old mill pond, which was completely silted up, has been reclaimed. The water supply is now controlled by Thames Water.

Other Services

Gas was supplied to the villages from 1925 and **electricity** from 1929.

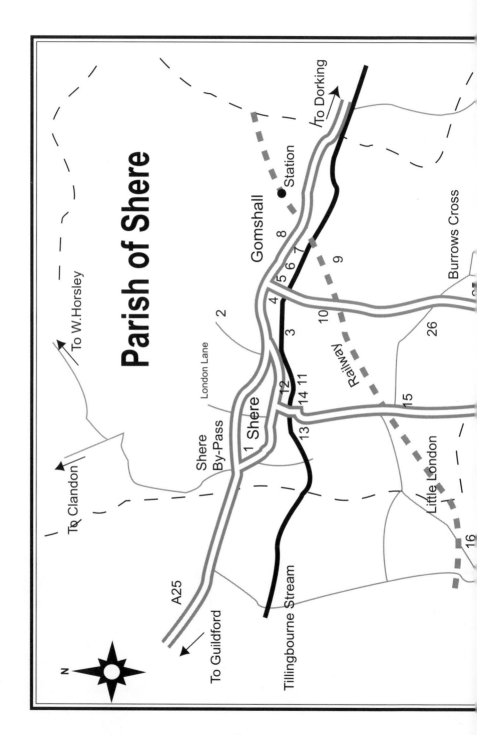

Parish of Shere

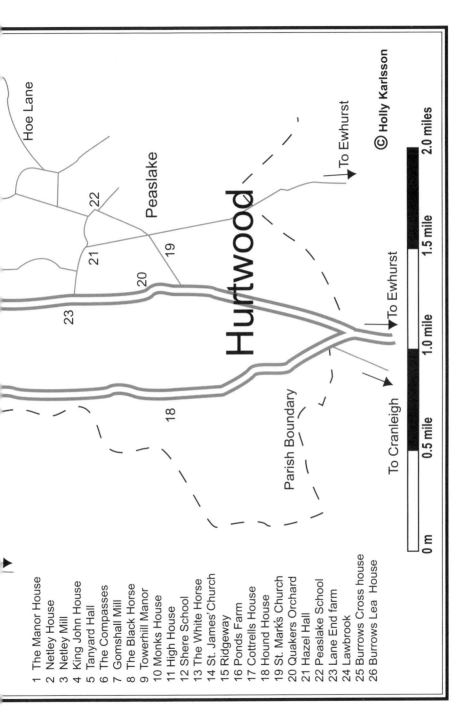

Hoe Lane

Peaslake

22

21

19

20

23

18

Hurtwood

Parish Boundary

To Ewhurst

To Ewhurst

To Cranleigh

© Holly Karlsson

| 0 m | 0.5 mile | 1.0 mile | 1.5 mile | 2.0 miles |

1 The Manor House
2 Netley House
3 Netley Mill
4 King John House
5 Tanyard Hall
6 The Compasses
7 Gomshall Mill
8 The Black Horse
9 Towerhill Manor
10 Monks House
11 High House
12 Shere School
13 The White Horse
14 St. James' Church
15 Ridgeway
16 Ponds Farm
17 Cottrells House
18 Hound House
19 St. Marks Church
20 Quakers Orchard
21 Hazel Hall
22 Peaslake School
23 Lane End farm
24 Lawbrook
25 Burrows Cross house
26 Burrows Lea House

INNS AND PUBLIC HOUSES

These have come and gone over the centuries. Before 1600, *The George* alehouse, said to have been a hostel for pilgrims, stood beside the churchyard. *The White Horse* in The Square has been an Inn since the 17th century. It was previously a farmhouse called Cripps and has traces of 14th century construction.

The White Horse, Shere

The original innkeepers at the *White Horse* were the Morgan Sherlocks from Wotton, about 1650–1730. Other families associated with the *White Horse* were the Hookers, Reffells and Farhalls and the Askews who managed it from 1866 to 1945.

Land adjoining it to the south was once a hop garden; *The Prince of Wales* (formerly Cook's beer shop) and the Maltings were built here in the mid 19th century.

Other inns are recorded. *The White Hart* (Willow Cottage) in Lower Street was in business in the 18th century and also *The Kings Arms,* part of the present Vine Cottages in Gomshall Lane.

In Gomshall, the *Black Horse* is recorded as an inn early in the 19th century. A malthouse was built about 1690 on this site and it later became a brewery that continued until 1925. The Reffells were owners of the *Black Horse* and the Brewery from 1812 to 1926. *The Compasses* started as a beershop built in 1830 which became an inn, in about 1886; both these establishments still serve the village of Gomshall. *The Hurtwood Inn* at Peaslake was built in 1920 on the site of two cottages; one of them was an off-licence belonging to Mr Voller.

The Black Horse, Gomshall

COMMUNICATIONS

The villages of Shere and Gomshall lie along the valley on the main route from Guildford to Dorking. On the ridge of the North Downs there was a cattle and sheep drove road, perhaps a section of an ancient trade route. The minor roads and lanes running south from Shere and Gomshall started as tracks between settlements, giving access to farms and into the Hurtwood, the Weald and beyond. Foot paths provided easy access between Albury, Shere and Gomshall. 'London Lane' is now a track leaving Upper Street between the Manor Lodge and the recreation ground; as its name suggests, it was once the main route to London. It is now bridged by the Shere by-pass, opened in 1960, which carries A25 traffic away from the centre of the village.

The Railway

The line between Guildford and Dorking, mainly along the Tillingbourne valley, was opened in 1849 by the Reading, Guildford and Reigate Railway Company. It was a part of the cross-country route planned "to secure through traffic passing between the west, north and midlands and the Channel ports, avoiding London". The site of a station to serve the villages might have been either at Gomshall or at Shere Heath. The Railway Company advertised that the place where the most passengers boarded or alighted on a given day would

Rail crash outside Gomshall Station, 1904

be the one chosen. It is said that Mr Acheson, the coal merchant at Gomshall, who was also the publican of the *Black Horse,* offered free beer to those supporting Gomshall. Whether or not this is true, the station was allotted to Gomshall.

Buses

The Trice family of Chilworth founded the Tillingbourne Valley Bus Company which, from 1924, ran a service from Guildford via Newlands Corner to Shere and Gomshall. This was later extended to Peaslake. The lower bus route connecting Guildford to Dorking via Albury which was started in 1914 by the Aldershot & District Traction Co., was continued by London & Country services and by the Tillingbourne Valley Company. Since 2001, services have been operated by Arriva, the routes being Guildford to Redhill via Dorking and Guildford to Cranleigh via Peaslake.

Post Offices

The first village post office in Shere was at Vaughan's from before 1871 until 1894. It was then transferred to the Surrey Trading Co., later the Forrest Stores. In the 1970s it was operated by Albert Cumper; from 1988 it was at Westleys, the Newsagents and returned to part of Speers (Alldays) in 2002. There was a Post Office in Gomshall Mill house and now a Post Office and general store is opposite Gomshall Mill. Peaslake has a post office and general store.

Telephones

There was a telephone at Shere post office in 1911 and a switchboard was subsequently installed, first at Grovers (Collins) and later at the barber's shop which is now a tea shop (The Lucky

VR post box in Shere

Duck). A Telephone Exchange was first built in Gomshall Lane in 1930 (now converted into flats), and a second one behind it in the 1960s.

SCHOOLS

Shere School

The earliest reference to education in Shere would appear to be an endowment of the interest from £120 in 2½ % Consolidated Stock. This was bequeathed in 1746, by the Rev. George Duncomb(e) for educational purposes. In 1758, Thomas Gatton bequeathed the interest on £400 for "teaching poor children to read and write". This latter legacy was sufficient to pay four teachers, two women and two men. It was normal at this time to teach only boys but Shere seems to have been rather enlightened as the names of some of the early pupils indicate that at least as many girls as boys benefitted from Thomas Gatton's will.

Shere School

Several dame schools and Sunday schools, charging a small fee, would also have provided a basic education.

Thomas Duncomb(e), the Rector for much of the first half of the 19th century, was not in favour of education for the poor but age and ill health obliged him to employ a curate. At about this time Miss Louisa Bray returned to live in Shere and she and Miss Laura Lomax decided to try to create a school. They found the new curate, the Rev. Handford, supportive of the idea and the three started a Sunday school. When a cottage belonging to Edmund Lomax became available, they used it to establish a weekday school, employing a master and mistress whose wages were funded by public subscription. The two ladies then turned their attention to raising funds and erecting a school and Master's house. The land and stone were donated by Edward Bray, the timber by Edmund Lomax and the building work was also funded by public subscription. This first purpose-built school was opened in 1842 and the church bells were rung in celebration. The first building was of local stone and in the centre of the site in Gomshall Lane. By 1845/47 it accommodated, on two floors, 86 boys and 66 girls on weekdays and on Sundays 126 boys and 86 girls. In about 1856 a new brick-built classroom was erected to the west and about 1870 another to the east to accommodate increasing numbers. Most local children were educated here until school leaving age unless they gained a scholarship to go elsewhere.

During the Second World War, the villages accepted evacuee children. Their education was continued at Shere by their own teachers, alternating class room space with local children.

From 1948 the school's official name was 'Shere Church of England (Controlled) Primary Mixed and Infants School'. It is a now styled 'The Shere Church of England Infant School'.

Peaslake School

The first school was opened in 1878 at the Mission Room which had been built in 1870 for church services. Mrs Harriet Grote of Ridgeway, Hook Lane, almost certainly arranged for the Mission Room to be built on land given by Augusta and Rosa Spottiswoode. Today, this property is known as the Old School Room and is used for local meetings.

By 1912 it had become obvious that this building could no longer accommodate the increasing number of pupils so a new, larger school was built on Colman's Hill at a site donated by Mr Fraser MacKenzie of Netley Park. Mr Frederick Blackburne of Hazel Hall was the principal benefactor of the building. The Bishop of Winchester dedicated this church school on 8th February 1913. A new wing was added by Mrs Blackburne-Hall in August 1929, in memory of her husband. Government education policy caused the school to close as a local authority church school in July 1994. However, Peaslake villagers insisted they keep their school and during negotiations with the church to obtain the building, classes were held at Ridgmont, Lawbrook Lane, home of Leslie and Margaret Jones. The school was re-opened in June 1997 and continues to flourish outside the state system.

Gypsy School
The 'wildlands' of the Hurtwood south of the villages had for centuries provided a place for gypsy camps. In 1926, a school especially for gypsy and traveller children was opened on land provided by the Bray estate near Wicket's Well. The master, Mr Milner, who had learned to speak the Romany language, lived in a caravan on the site. The corrugated iron classroom was designed to be portable and in 1934 it was transferred to Walton-on-Thames, where the families were resettled.

The Gypsy School

VILLAGE HALLS and LEISURE AMENITIES
The original Shere Parish Hall was built to celebrate the Diamond Jubilee of Queen Victoria. The first sod of the foundations was turned on Jubilee Day, 22nd June 1897 and the building was opened on 5th August 1898. The site for the hall was a gift from Colonel Fraser of Netley and the money for the building was raised by local fund-raising events and donations.

Shere Village Hall

A second hall was built beside the first and opened in December 1922 to commemorate victory in the First World War. Once again, funds were raised by local people. The original hall was converted into the Shere Men's Social Club. The Shere Club, as it became known, closed after 74 years on 5th January 1997. Since April 1999, the greater part of this building has been leased to a nursery school.

Peaslake Memorial Hall

During the Second World War the Red Cross Room at the rear of the first building was destroyed by a bomb. The Memorial Hall was built in its place and opened in 1951.
The Memorial Hall in **Peaslake** was presented to the community by the Misses Spottiswoode in 1923.

From 2002 there has been a hall for community use in **Gomshall**. This is a 16th century timber-framed building, once used as offices by Gomshall Tannery and known as 'Jordells' in old deeds. As part of the 'planning gain' following the development of the tannery site for housing, the building was renovated and is now owned and administered by Shere Parish Council. The name, chosen by local vote, is 'Tanyard Hall'.

Recreation Grounds
In 1925, land for the **Shere** Recreation Ground was purchased by public subscription. It lies behind the Village Halls and is administered by trustees.
In **Gomshall,** the Goose Green recreation grounds are leased from the Bray Manor Estate by the Parish Council.
Peaslake has the use of the field behind the village school (formerly a church school), which is leased by the Parish Council from the Diocese of Guildford.

The Swimming Pool
The "open bathing place" in the field to the east of Shere school was presented to the community in 1891 by Lady Arthur Russell of The Ridgeway, Hook Lane, herself an enthusiastic swimmer. It is considered to be one of the earliest open-air public swimming pools in the country and it has survived several threats of closure. After some ninety years of administration by the Parish Council the pool has, since 1989, been leased to 'The Shere Swimming Pool Club'.

The Museum and Archives
Shere Museum began in 1984 as a one-day event, part of the 'Fair in the Square' to raise funds for the Shere Village Hall. The Museum, located at the Old Malthouse in Shere Lane, established regular opening and continues to this day.
The research room contains much useful archival material for anyone interested in Shere parish or local families.

Shere Museum

The Local History Society records are also housed here.

Some Lost Pleasures

Theatricals

Records of home-grown entertainments tend to be ephemeral, but those for amateur theatricals in the parish throughout the twentieth century show an active local involvement in music and drama. Crispin Hill, for example, son of the then rector of Shere, wrote and produced several pantomimes and other stage pieces between 1911 and 1919. Charles Whittington, a local piano teacher, contributed the music for several of these works.

The Barn Theatre

Community pageants dramatising the (somewhat romanticised) history of the villages were produced, notably in 1925 and 1977. The Shere and Peaslake Boy Scouts ran their 'gang shows'. Village choirs competed in the annual Leith Hill Festivals (Shere from 1905, Peaslake from 1912) and the Peaslake Operatic and Dramatic Society flourished during the inter-war years. 1948 saw the creation of not only the Shere and Gomshall Dramatic Society (which ceased in the 1960s) but also of the Peaslake Players, who give popular performances to this day.

From 1932 to 1939, a barn at High House Farm provided the 'Barn Theatre' venue for the 'Otherwise Club', some of whose performers later became famous. Peter Ustinov and Herbert Lom are the most notable. The story of this venture is told in *Otherwise a Barn* (see page 31).

Shere Bonfire

In 1878, Shere village organised a bonfire celebration for Guy Fawkes night. They can have had little idea what they were starting. The bonfire became an annual event and grew into a huge carnival, drawing crowds from far and wide, and raising money for many charities. In 1938, the 'Bonfire Boys' (the popular name of the Shere United Bonfire Association), organised a Diamond Jubilee. They were not to know this was to be the last celebration for some years, but the Second World War intervened.

To give an indication of how the simple bonfire had developed, in 1938 the programme included a procession consisting of "pedestrians in fancy costume, decorated cycles, decorated hand trucks, private cars and tableau vehicles". The procession was headed by the Band of the Royal Air Force and the Drums and Fifes of the Queen's Royal Regiment.

Programme

SHERE BONFIRE CARNIVAL

(IN AID OF THE ROYAL SURREY COUNTY AND OTHER HOSPITALS)

will be held at

Shere, on Saturday, Nov. 6th, 1937

6.30 p.m.   THE PROCESSION

HEADED BY

THE BAND OF THE 318th A.A. COMPANY ROYAL ENGINEERS, T.A.

(*By kind permission of the Officers commanding*)

And consisting of **Pedestrians in Fancy Costumes** **Decorated Cycles and Hand Trucks and Tableau Vehicles**

Will form in the LOWER STREET, SHERE.

7 p.m. The Procession will move off and proceed through The Square, Spinning Walk, Middle Street and Gomshall Lane, to the Black Horse Hotel, Gomshall, where it will be met by the Peaslake Procession headed by the DAGENHAM GIRL PIPERS.

The procession went from Shere to Gomshall, 'paused' at the *Black Horse,* and marched back again. Meanwhile a large funfair was opened on Shere recreation ground. At 8.30 the giant bonfire was lit by a torch which had been carried by runners in relay from the Royal Surrey County Hospital (by then the major recipient of donations), with a firework display at 9.00. There was parking for 1500 cars (you wonder where in Shere!), directed by the Automobile Association and special late buses were run to Guildford. It wasn't until 1951 that the Bonfire Boys lit their next bonfire and the celebrations continued to get bigger and better. By 1953 it had become normal to have four bands leading the procession. Sadly, all good things must come to an end and some time in the 1960s the fun stopped. The event had become too big and hooligan elements were causing increasing problems. The Bonfire Boys disbanded and a tradition died.

SOME HISTORICAL ASSOCIATIONS
The villages in the parish of Shere have been concerned with their rural pursuits for most of their long history, but just occasionally national events impinged upon them.

In 1258 there was an affray in the churchyard which became known as **'The Battle of Shere'**. The ownership of the advowson* of Shere church was in contention between the powerful baron John Fitzgeoffrey, Lord of the manor, and the Abbot of Netley who was supported by the bishop-elect of Winchester, half brother to King Henry III. There was fighting and bloodshed, one Shere man died.
Later in that year, there was a political revolution in parliament with the barons pressing for reforms to limit the power of the king. Events in Shere are thought to have triggered a new stage in the confrontation between the barons and the crown.

In the time of Queen Elizabeth I, when war with Spain seemed likely, a force of 150 able-bodied men of the parish of Shere was mustered in readiness. In 1588 Captain Richard Hill of Sutton Place led this company to London to help guard against the threat from **the Spanish Armada.**
During the **English Civil War** a subsequent owner of Sutton Place, Richard Holman, a London lawyer, is recorded as subscribing to a loan to King Charles I. Arthur Haughton of Lawbrook was "a long time servant to His Majesty (Charles I) in the office of His Majesty's works". This demonstrated local Royalist sympathies, but Surrey on the whole, and so probably the majority of Shere residents, supported Parliament in the Civil War.

In 1741 **the Foundling Hospital** was opened in London, the initiative of Thomas Coram, retired sea captain and trader, shocked at the number of babies abandoned and left to die on the streets of the capital. The need was so great that, as well as accommodating the children at the hospital, they were sent to villages around London. Organisers were appointed to recruit nursing mothers and bring them by wagon to collect the babies and take them home. They were rewarded with a monthly wage and a supply of baby clothes. In the Shere burial register, the deaths of 43 'foundlings' are recorded between 1758 and 1790; so far, only two have been identified who returned to the Foundling Hospital at the age of five to receive an education and an apprenticeship.

24

Burials showing Foundlings 1758	
Jan 4	The wife of George Eastmund (tanner)
Mar 4	Ann Holland, widow of John Holland senior
Mar 31	The Widow Holmes
Apr 12	The Widow Simonds from Sussex (fee for burial 6/8d)
May 17	William Bromley, inf. From Foundling Hospital
May 19	Thomas Russell
Jun 3	The wife of Richard Dowling
Jun 6	William Drax, infant from the Foundling Hospital
Jun 27	The wife of Wm White (taylor)
Aug 21	Sarah Edsar
Sep 2	George Beadle, foundling
Sep 3	Grace Miller, foundling
Sep 19	John Deroant, foundling

Gomshall's contribution to national history is an incident in 1888 when William **Gladstone,** the Prime Minister, was intercepted on his way to Gomshall station from visiting the Leveson-Gower's in Holmbury St Mary. He was presented with a telegram concerning a crisis in Montenegro and asked to write a reply. This he did, at the *Black Horse.*

Eighteenth and nineteenth century Peaslake had a reputation for being on the **smugglers'** route from the coast to London, offering hiding places in remote wooded areas, an activity which, by its nature, is hard to prove. Early 20th century Peaslake was said to be a "nest of **suffragettes**", containing "fourteen ladies of very advanced views". In May 1914, the house 'Brackenside' offered Mrs Emmeline Pankhurst a "secret country retreat".

The losses of men in the **World Wars** of the 20th century are commemorated by the War Memorial Crosses that stand in Shere and Peaslake. There are the names of 33 men of Shere and Gomshall who died in 1914–1918 and 20 who died in 1939–1945. Peaslake records fatalities of 17 men in World War I and 12 men in World War 2.

Shere War Memorial

Peaslake War Memorial

DEVELOPMENTS SINCE 1850

The years 1850 to the present have seen enormous changes in the villages, not so much in their physical appearance as in the structure, lifestyle and outlook of the population.

In 1850, most agricultural methods and skills were similar to those practised several hundred years before and a high proportion of employed men worked on the land. Now, very little is grown locally for local use, most of the farmland being meadow or pasture and providing very little employment.

In 1850, the monied few lived lives apart from the majority of the population: now the divisions are less absolute.

Prior to 1850, the commonest modes of travel were on horseback or on foot. The coming of the railway in 1849 widened horizons for the local population and began to bring new residents and visitors to the villages. Towards the end of the nineteenth century artists were drawn by the natural beauty of the landscape; some made their homes here. In the 1920s and 30s, Shere, Gomshall and Peaslake were 'discovered' by tourists and became popular venues for cyclists, motorcyclists, motorists and hikers. Now the number of cars driving through or parked in the streets means freedom of movement to some, irritation to others.

In 1850, the officers of the parish vestry collected and distributed rates for the repair of the highways, the support of the poor and the provision of a constable: from the late nineteenth century these services have been provided by parish, borough and county councils and central government.

From 1850 until after the Second World War, the villages were largely self-sufficient for daily needs and there was a strong sense of community and an active involvement in a wide range of local activities. Now there is little local employment and the majority of the working population (and schoolchildren over the age of seven) drive (or are driven) to work or place of education at some distance from their homes.

Shere, Gomshall and Peaslake are still good places to live, though high house prices make it hard for young people to stay close to home. There is a mix of long term residents and incomers; clubs, societies and churches offer interest and companionship to all age groups. Houses in the villages built several hundred years ago for a very different society have been adapted for present needs and are cherished and enjoyed by residents and visitors alike.

NOTABLE PEOPLE ASSOCIATED WITH THE VILLAGES

ALLINGHAM Helen (1848–1926) and William (1824–1889)
Helen was an artist of Surrey rural life. In 1878 they rented The Cottage in Upper Street and used Workshop Cottage in Rectory Lane as a studio. William was a once-popular poet.

BRAY William (1736–1832)
Lord of the manor of Shere, he lived at Hawkins (now Old Manor Cottages) in Upper Street during the latter half of his long life. He amplified the notes left by Rev. Owen Manning to form the 3-volume *History and Antiquities of the County of Surrey* (1804–1814) which is still a classic of county history.

BARRIE Sir J.M. (1860–1937)
The author of *Peter Pan* (1904) and many other plays and novels stayed at Anchor Cottage in Upper Street during the 1890s. He once organised a cricket team (including Conan Doyle and other authors and artists) which played against the Shere village XI. According to Barrie's memoirs, the poet and novelist George **MEREDITH** (1828–1909), later to be one of the 'Sunday Tramps' whose rambles included this area, lodged, while a young man, over a butcher's shop in Shere.

BOULT Sir Adrian (1889–1983)
The renowned orchestral conductor owned Quakers in Peaslake from 1933 to 1944.

COLE Sir Henry (1808–1888)
He was the first Director of the Victoria & Albert Museum and his suggestion to John Callcott Horsley resulted in the first commercial Christmas card in 1843. He rented and converted Seaforth Cottage, Gomshall Lane, 1856–1860.

GILBERT Sir Alfred (1854–1934)
A sculptor whose most familiar work is the statue of Eros in Piccadilly Circus, he lived at Monks House in Gomshall (then called Gravel Pits) in the 1890s.

GROTE George (1794–1871)
An eminent banker, radical M.P. and author of a standard history of Greece, he lived at The Ridgeway, Hook Lane, from 1866. His wife Harriet (1792–1878) was a writer and musician and hostess to artists.

HOPGOOD Flt. Lt. JV 'Hoppy' DFC and Bar (1921–1943)
In 1943, 'Hoppy', late of Hurstcote (replaced by Shere Court), piloted his Lancaster bomber on the famous Dambusters (617 Squadron) raid . He was killed attacking the Meohne dam.

HYDE William (1859–1925)
An artist and book illustrator, he lived from 1895 at Sayers, The Square, with his wife Kate **ROGERS** (1861–1942) a designer and decorator of Doulton vases. (Sir Henry Doulton had a house south of Peaslake).

LAUGHTON Charles (1899–1962)
and his wife Elsa **LANCHESTER** (1902–1986) had a country cottage at Stapledown, north of Shere, in the 1930s and frequented the village (see Williams-Ellis below).

LEADER Benjamin Williams (1831–1923).
This landscape painter lived from 1888 at Burrows Cross House which was designed by Norman **SHAW** in 1885 for the artist Frank **HOLL** (1845–1888).

LLOYD Percy (1865–1946)
One of Britain's earliest picture postcard photographers and publishers, he was born in Upper Street (thought to be at the house called Denmarke) and worked from a studio in Albury.

LUTYENS Sir Edwin (1869–1944)
This architect stayed as a guest at Shere Manor, Sir Reginald Bray having commissioned him to design a shop in Middle Street (1892), the eastern lodge of the manor house, a pair of cottages in Upper Street (1894) and later the lych gate at St. James' Church (1902).

MARRIOTT-WATSON
This family settled in Shere and included:- Henry Brereton (died in Shere 1922), novelist; Rosamund, his wife, poet; Frank (H.B.'s brother), playwright; his wife Florence, actress and their daughter Nan, actress, broadcaster and playwright.

MARTIN Leonard (1869–1936)
An architect whose local work includes the former British Legion Hall and 'Hazel Hatch' at Peaslake and in London, the Girl Guides Association Headquarters (1926). He lived at Hoe Farm, Peaslake, before building Martins (now Little Brook), Sutton Abinger, in 1933.

NORTON Charles Goodwin (1856–1940)
He was born at Anchor Cottage, Upper Street and produced short 'Moving Pictures' as early as 1898. He is now internationally recognised as a pioneer of cinematography.

PETHICK-LAWRENCE Lord Frederick (1871–1961)
He was a leading Labour politician and a staunch supporter of the Women's Suffrage Movement, of which his first wife (Emmeline Pethick) was the treasurer. Their country retreat was, from 1922, a cottage in Rad Lane between Gomshall and Peaslake.

READ Ernest (1879–1965)
He was born at Seaforth Cottage, Gomshall Lane, a musician and musical educationalist instigating the Youth Orchestra movement and founding the Ernest Read Concerts for Children.

TARRANT Margaret (1888–1959)
An artist and illustrator, famous for her pictures of flowers, fairies and children. She lived first at Gomshall then at Peaslake until shortly before her death.

WILLIAMS-ELLIS Clough (1883–1978)
An architect, best known for Portmeirion village in North Wales. He designed several houses in this locality, including, in the 1920s, a ground level 'tree-house', at Stapledown, off the Shere-East Clandon road (see Laughton, above). He then built a neighbouring cottage as a larger country retreat for himself and his wife.

GLOSSARY (Words marked * in the text)

Advowson Originally the patronage of an ecclesiastical house or benefice, now the right of presentation to a **benefice** (an ecclesiastical living).

Anchoress A woman who has withdrawn from the world for religious reasons.

Attainder Loss of civil rights and forfeiture of estate, rank or title, following a sentence of death.

Bordar A villein cottager and one of the lowest ranks in feudal society.

Demesne lands Land retained by the Lord of the manor for his own use and upon which tenants gave free service according to the custom of the manor.

Early English English gothic architectural style of the 13th century. Pointed arches replaced the heavy rounded Norman ones.

Eboracum/Eborum The Latin name of York.

Fifteenths and Tenths A 'Lay Subsidy' or a tax on a person's moveable items, estimated at a tenth of the value of goods for town dwellers and a fifteenth for country dwellers. Last collected in 1623.

Fuller/Fulling A man engaged in fulling cloth. Fulling cloth, a process which cleanses and thickens the material by treading or beating it.

Fustian A napped fabric of a mixture of linen and cotton or wool.

Greensand Geological term for a type of sandstone found in the Tillingbourne valley and elsewhere.

Hide Originally the amount of land which could be cultivated in a year with one ox-team of eight oxen. Usually considered to hold four **virgates.** Also used as a tax unit in the Domesday survey.

Hundred An administrative division of a shire, probably established in the 10th century.

Mercer A member of the Mercers' Livery Company: a dealer in cloth.

Perpendicular Late style of English Gothic architecture, late 15th to mid 16th centuries.

Rood A name generally applied to the large cross above the entrance to the chancel in pre-reformation and Roman Catholic churches.

Transitional An architectural term referring to the period of building between the Norman style and Early English gothic (12th century).

Vill A division of the hundred; a tax-paying unit at Domesday and the 1380 Poll Tax.

Villein A general term used to describe an unfree tenant after the Norman conquest.

Virgate or Yardland A variable measure of land, depending on the quality of the soil. Considered to be one quarter of a **hide.**

SOURCES OF INFORMATION

Primary Sources

At Shere Museum

The Arts file: artists and theatricals

Bonfire Boys: file

Dr Isaac Cory: files

District Nursing Association (Shere): Minute Book 1908 - 1952

Gypsy school: file

Houses and Farmlands: expanded notes by Sir J Sutherland-Harris

Manors of Shere & Gomshall: Typescript by Sir J Sutherland-Harris 1975

Parish Hall / Club: file

Parish Magazines since 1895

Roman Catholic Church at Gomshall: Account by Pat Packer 1995

Shere School: A History, by Bevis Colmer (1992)

Shere & Gomshall WI Scrapbooks, 1949 and 1965

Swimming Pool: file

Tradesmen & Craftsman of Shere 1600-1900, Typescript by
  Sir J Sutherland-Harris 1973

At Surrey History Centre

Book of Reckonings: Psh/Sher 10/1

Diaries of William Bray:

Manor Records (numerous)

Parish Registers: (some transcripts at Museum)

Will of David Harris, miller, 1786 G85/13/73

At National Archives (PRO)

Gladstone's letter (copy at Museum)

Poll Tax 1380 for Shere and Gomshall E179/184.29 (transcript at Museum)

Will of Arthur Haughton of Lawbrook Prob11/375/Q43

At London Metropolitan Archives

Extensive records of the Coram Foundation (Foundling Hospital)

Maps

Map of Surrey; Emmanuel Bowen 1753

Copies of Bray Estate maps, 1772, 1827 and 1829

Secondary Sources Local Booklets and Journals

Book of Reckonings (extracts) *and other memoranda 1500 - 1612;*
Christine Carpenter; History of St James' Church, pub. Shere Parochial
Church Council, available in church

About the Hurtwood, The Hurtwood Control Committee (1991)

Old Houses in the Parish of Shere (1976/2003); *A Tannery in Gomshall*
(1997/2003); *The Tillingbourne Story* (1984/2003); published by the Shere,
Gomshall & Peaslake Local History Society

Old Village Houses in Shere and Gomshall by Sir Jack Sutherland-Harris
in *Surrey History* Vol I Nos 1 & 2 (1973, 1974)

The Poll Tax in Shere and Gomshall, Ann Noyes in *Surrey History* Vol. VI
Nos 3 & 4 (2001, 2002)

Otherwise a Barn, Joan Mant, Hazeltree Publishing (1999)
Shere Poverty, Ann Noyes, Twiga Books, (1996)
Shere and its Rectors, Granville Leveson Gower, in *Surrey Archaeological Collections* Vol. VIII (1883)
Shere: a Surrey Village in Maps Shere, Gomshall & Peaslake LHS, Surrey Archaeological Society (2001)
A Suffragette Nest, Jenny Overton and Joan Mant, Hazeltree Publishing (1998)
What happened at Shere? (Battle of Shere), Dr Susan Stewart in *Southern History* Vol. 22, (2000)

Other Secondary Sources

Domesday Book, Surrey, John Morris and Sara Wood, Phillimore, (1975)
Dorking Railways, Alan Jackson, Dorking Local History Group, (1988)
Dictionary of National Biography, History & Antiquities of the County of Surrey, Owen Manning & William Bray, 3 Vols, (1804 - 1814)
The Local History of England, WG Hoskins, Longmans (1953/84)
Natural History & Antiquities of the County of Surrey, John Aubrey (1718-19)
Place Names of Surrey, JEB Gover et al, CUP (1934/69)
Surrey Musters 1584/85 in *Surrey Record Society* Vol III No 2 (1914)
Tillingbourne: the Tillingbourne Bus Story, George Burnett & Laurie James Middleton Press (1990)
Victoria County History of England (Surrey), HE Malden ed., 4 Vols, (1904 - 1914)

Grateful thanks are due to everyone who has contributed additional information during our research.

The illustrations are taken from the archives and library at Shere Museum.

FURTHER READING

Surrey Books

A History of Surrey, Peter Brandon, Phillimore (1977/98)
Surrey: A County History, John Janaway, Countryside Books, (1994)

Some Other Titles which include a reference to Shere

Rural Rides, William Cobbett (1830)
The Greenwood Hat, JM Barrie (1937)
The Old Road, Hilaire Belloc (1904)